GW

Teen Agency Program (Y.A.P.)
Allen County Public Library

D1259562

Tween Prayer

Other Church Publishing Books by Nancy Roth

We Sing of God: A Hymnal for Children (1989)
Robert N. Roth and Nancy L. Roth, editors (Teacher's Guide,
Children's Hymnbook, Rudiments of Music Worksheets, and Audiotape)

Praying: A Book for Children (1991)
A Closer Walk: Meditating on Hymns for Year A (1998)
Awake My Soul: Meditating on Hymns for Year B (1999)
New Every Morning: Meditating on Hymns for Year C (2000)
Praise My Soul: Meditating on Hymns (2001) Large print edition

Coming from Church Publishing in 2005:
An Invitation to Christian Yoga (book and CD)

Also by Nancy Roth
Meditations for Choir Members (Morehouse, 1999)
Organic Prayer (Cowley, 1993)
The Breath of God (Cowley, 2002)

Nancy Roth

Tween Prayer

Friendship with God

Church Publishing • New York

Copyright © 2004 Nancy Roth

All rights reserved.

A catalog record of this book is available from the Library of Congress

ISBN 0-89869-395-0

Church Publishing Incorporated
445 Fifth Avenue
New York, NY 10016

www.churchpublishing.org

To Molly and all the others

Acknowledgments

I owe a debt to a retreat participant, whose name I have long forgotten, who first expressed the need for a book for young adolescents similar to *Praying: A Book for Children*, which I wrote for children of elementary-school age. That book was a young child's version of my book *The Breath of God*. This one is for young women at the threshold of the journey to adulthood, an exhilarating period when the spiritual seeds that come their way find especially fertile soil.

As always, I also thank my first editor, supporter, and beloved companion of forty-five years, my husband Bob.

I am grateful to those others who also read and critiqued the manuscript: Jacob Mercer, Sam Mercer, Molly Murphy, Susan McDonald, and the Rev. Anita Schell-Lambert. Their helpful comments have shaped the final version of this book.

Contents

What Is Praying? 1

Praying with Words 7

Praying by Thinking about God 20

Praying by Silent Listening 28

Praying in Work and in Play 35

Temples of the Holy Spirit 57

Praying All Day Long 67

What Is Praying?

This book is for you, the young women who are journeying toward adulthood. Your parents probably have told you stories about how much the world has changed since they were your age. When you become adults, you will probably tell similar stories to the young people you know, because the world will continue to change, becoming smaller and more complex at the same time. Fortunately, you will not be alone on your journey into the future. You will have the support and friendship of God.

This book is about the way this friendship grows through praying. When I was young, I learned in Sunday school that "praying is talking with God." As I grew up, I began to discover that praying is much more than that; in fact, I realized that I was already praying in other ways. Praying includes all the ways that we grow in friendship with God, not just the talking ways. Can you imagine talking nonstop to a friend? I would guess that your friend would get sick of it really fast. Talking with God is part of our praying, but it isn't the only part.

The better you know your friends, for example, the more likely you are to *think* about them—even when you are not actually together. "Hmmm, I wonder what Jessica is doing on this rainy day. I wonder whether Jason passed the history test. Why did Heather seem sad when I saw her at lunch? Didn't Sam do a great job getting my email to work?" Thinking about our friends is a sign of our friendship.

Another way to help our friendship grow is to *work* with our friends. It's fun to work together on a school newspaper, to plant a garden in a vacant lot, to help serve meals in a soup kitchen, to play basketball or another team sport, or to work for a recycling program in your neighborhood. You get to know friends better when you work beside them.

The better you know someone, the more you are able to *listen* to them, rather than fill up all the time with your own talking. Then you really notice what they are thinking and what they are feeling. Sometimes you can just sit together silently, maybe on the front steps of your house or apartment on a hot summer day, watching the clouds in the sky and listening to the birds in the trees or the noises of the busy city.

There are many ways we can grow closer to our friends. From your own experience, you know that friendship can grow through thinking about the people you like, working with them, listening to them, or just hanging out, not doing much of anything.

I believe that this is true also of our friendship with God. We can, of course, talk to God. But we can also think about God. We can do God's work. We can simply be silent and remember that God is with us. All of these ways of growing closer to God are ways of praying.

Sometimes life is so busy or painful that it is easy to forget our friendship with God. We may even wonder if God likes us very much. But God never forgets you. And God never stops loving you. Throughout your life, nothing will give you more strength, peace, comfort, and joy than your friendship with God. God is a friend who will be there for you, forever.

Using This Book as a Journal

As you read this book, you may want to write or draw some of the ideas that come to you. It can become your own "prayer book" in which you can write your thoughts and prayers. We have left blank pages throughout this book as a way for you to get started. We have also made some suggestions of what you might like to think about.

Someday in the future, you might want to buy a blank notebook in order to continue this project. Some people call this a journal. (This word comes from the French word for "day," which is *jour*.) Some people actually do write in their journals every day, and some people just write in them whenever they feel like it. Many people discover that these journals are like faithful friends, who help them think through problems and help them in their ongoing conversation with God.

Journal Pages

Think of your best friend.

How did you meet?

How did you get to know him or her better?

What are some of the ways that your friendship continues to grow?

_____

_____

_____

_____

_____

_____

_____

_____

_____

_____

_____

_____

_____

_____

_____

_____

_____

_____

_____

Pictures and Drawings

- 2 -

Praying with Words

"Talking prayer" is not just saying words: it is sharing all your thoughts with God. When you talk with your best friends, you probably find that you can be very honest. You share with them the things that make you angry or sad, as well as the things that make you happy. The same is true with God, with one important difference. You can tell God everything, even things you wouldn't tell your best friend. God will not laugh at you, ignore you, or judge you—no matter what.

Prayers from the Bible

There are prayers from the Bible that help you think of the things you want to tell God. These prayers were originally prayed in Hebrew, Aramaic, and Greek, the languages of the people who wrote them. The prayers we use from the Bible are translations into English, and different people have translated them in different ways. For example, when Jesus' friends asked him, "Lord, teach us to pray," he taught them the prayer called the Lord's Prayer. You may know a version of the Lord's Prayer that is different from the one in this book, but it is the same prayer Jesus gave us, and small differences in what we say don't change that. The Lord's Prayer has always been the favorite prayer of Christians because it includes many things we want to share with God:

Our Father in heaven, hallowed be your Name, your kingdom come, your will be done, on earth as in heaven.

These words mean that we believe that God is holy ("hallowed") and that we hope the earth will be the place God intended it to be, where people live in harmony and peace with one another and the world of nature.

Give us today our daily bread.

We ask God for the things we need in order to live, such as bread (or enough food). When we pray this, we can think also of people in the world who do not have enough to eat, or who don't have homes, or jobs, or other material necessities of life.

Forgive us our sins as we forgive those who sin against us.

When we say these words, we tell God that we are sorry if we have hurt other people in any way (even if we don't realize it), and also that we want to forgive people who have hurt us. Forgiving people who have hurt us is really hard to do—so hard we can't do it without God's help.

Save us from the time of trial, and deliver us from evil.

We ask God's help in keeping us from wanting to do things that harm us or other people, and we ask for God's protection from harm and from the temptations we face every day.

For the kingdom, the power, and the glory are yours, now and for ever. Amen.

Worshipers added this phrase long ago to the biblical version of the Lord's Prayer. The words speak of God's "kingdom," which was a major theme of Jesus' preaching. It is a kingdom of love, justice, and peace. When you read the headlines, when you think about terrorism and war, it is very obvious that such a kingdom has not yet arrived. However, Christians hope, work, and pray for a world in which God's "kingdom, power, and glory" will reign. The very last word in many prayers, "Amen," means "I want it to be this way" in the Hebrew language in which many of our prayers were first written.

There are many other prayers in the Bible, such as Mary's prayer called "The Magnificat." Mary said this prayer after the angel Gabriel told her she would be the mother of Jesus. You can find this prayer if you look in the Gospel of Luke in the first chapter, verses 46–55.

My soul magnifies the Lord,
and my spirit rejoices in God my Savior,
for he has regarded the low estate of his handmaiden.
For behold, henceforth all generations will call me blessed;
for he who is mighty has done great things for me,
and holy is his name.
And his mercy is on those who fear him,
from generation to generation.
He has shown strength with his arm,
he has scattered the proud in the imagination of their hearts,
he has put down the mighty from their thrones,
and exalted those of low degree;
he has filled the hungry with good things,
and the rich he has sent empty away.
He has helped his servant Israel,
in remembrance of his mercy,
as he spoke to our father,
to Abraham and to his posterity forever.

In this prayer, Mary says her soul "magnifies" the Lord. Have you ever looked through a magnifying glass and seen something that is usually almost invisible, like a grain of sand, become very large? Just as a magnifying glass makes things become larger—or "greater"—Mary "magnified" God by praising God's greatness.

I can picture Mary actually singing this prayer. She sang about how amazing it was that God had chosen someone who was poor, or of "low estate," to be the mother of Jesus. God could have chosen a great princess from a royal family. It was as if the world were turned upside-down. Instead of giving special gifts to people who were proud, mighty, and rich, God gave them to people who were humble, powerless, and hungry. Mary remembered that, long ago, God had promised blessings to her ancestor Abraham and his descendents. Now she knew it was true.

There is also a whole prayer book in the Bible, called the book of Psalms. The Psalms—150 of them—were written long before Jesus was born, so that they were part of Jesus' prayer book too. They were originally sung to the music of an instrument called a "psaltery." It had strings (no one is sure exactly how many) that were plucked to accompany the person singing the prayer. If you have a guitar, harp, or other stringed instrument, you can pluck it as you make up your own tunes to a psalm.

The Twenty-third Psalm is a favorite prayer about God's care for us. You have probably heard it at a funeral, where it offers great comfort to people who have lost a loved one. You can find out about this Psalm translation, as well as other books I will mention in *Tween Prayer*, in the Notes on the last page of this book.

*The Holy One is my shepherd; ***
I shall not be in want.
*You make me lie down in green pastures ***
and lead me beside still waters.
*You revive my soul ***
and guide me along right pathways for the sake of your Name.
Though I walk through the valley of the shadow of death,

*I shall fear no evil; ***
for you are with me;
your rod and your staff, they comfort me.
*You spread a table before me in the presence of those who trouble me; ***
you have anointed my head with oil,
and my cup is running over.
*Surely your goodness and mercy shall follow me all the days of my life, ***
and I will dwell in the house of God forever. [1]

This prayer compares God to a shepherd who helps his sheep find green grass to eat and fresh water to drink, guides them along the right paths, and protects them from danger. In fact, God loves us so much that it seems as if God is giving a party for us—spreading out food on a table and pouring so much into our drinking cup that it overflows. At the time the psalms were written, one of the things people did to welcome guests was to pour sweet perfumed oil on their heads, which was called "anointing" their heads with oil.

This is a very helpful psalm to say when you are sad or afraid. It tells of the depth of God's care for us. You do indeed feel as if you are walking "through the valley of the shadow of death" when a person or relationship has changed or died. Perhaps you yourself are sick or afraid. Or maybe you have lost someone important to you—through death, a quarrel, separation, or a divorce. It is helpful to know God's healing presence is always with you, supporting you as you go through a difficult time.

There are other prayers that we say in church, such as the Sanctus. Sanctus is the Latin word for "holy," and that is just what it says:

Holy, holy, holy Lord, God of power and might,
heaven and earth are full of your glory.
Hosanna in the highest.

That prayer comes from the book of Isaiah in the Old Testament. In chapter 6, verse 3, you can read about the prophet Isaiah, who saw angels singing in the temple. When we say or sing the Sanctus, we are joining in the prayer of the angels. We add "Hosanna in the Highest," which is a way to ask God to be with us. Hosanna means "be our help" in Hebrew.

The Sanctus is usually followed by the Benedictus, which is simply the Latin way of saying "blessed":

Blessed is he who comes in the name of the Lord.
Hosanna in the highest.

This prayer is found in the Bible, too. Look in the New Testament for Matthew 21:9, where the people shout those words when Jesus enters the city of Jerusalem on Palm Sunday.

Prayers from Prayer Books

Other prayers were first prayed by people who lived after the Bible was written. For example, in some churches there is a beautiful prayer for Compline, a service for nighttime, said just before going to bed. This prayer was first used long ago in monasteries, communities where people gathered to live a life of worship and prayer. But it would be a wonderful prayer for everybody to say before going to sleep:

Guide us waking, O Lord, and guard us sleeping; that awake we may
watch with Christ, and asleep we may rest in peace.

When I say those words in a service, they make me feel so relaxed that it is sometimes difficult to keep from yawning. I guess you could call this prayer "instant stress reduction."

Another prayer in many prayer books is said to have been written by St. Francis of Assisi:

Lord, make us instruments of your peace.
Where there is hatred, let us sow love;

where there is injury, pardon;
where there is discord, union;
where there is doubt, faith;
where there is despair, hope;
where there is darkness, light;
where there is sadness, joy.
Grant that we may not so much seek to be consoled as to console;
to be understood as to understand;
to be loved as to love.
For it is in giving that we receive;
it is in pardoning that we are pardoned;
and it is in dying that we are born to eternal life. Amen.

That prayer is about the way of living shown by Jesus, which St. Francis followed too: a way of peace and love and giving rather than fighting, hating, and taking.

There are also some wonderful modern collections of prayers, such as *Earth Prayers, Life Prayers,* and *Peace Prayers,*[2] or *The Oxford Book of Prayer.*[3] Books like these contain prayers from many centuries, and they also contain prayers from other religious traditions, such as Buddhism, Hinduism, and Islam, and from the Native American tradition. An example from the Native American tradition is this Ojibway prayer, in which God is addressed as "Grandfather":

Grandfather,
Look at our brokenness.

We know that in all creation
Only the human family
Has strayed from the Sacred Way.

We know that we are the ones who are divided
And we are the ones

Who must come back together
To walk in the Sacred Way.

Grandfather,
Sacred One,
Teach us love, compassion, and honor
That we may heal the earth
And heal each other.[4]

When we say prayers from our Christian ancestors, whether at church or in our own home, we connect ourselves with what the church calls "the communion of saints"—all the Christians who have ever lived. When we say prayers from other traditions, we express our unity with others around the world who are seeking the same thing: God.

Grace

Some families pray together regularly at home. An example of this is grace at meals. The word "grace" comes for the Latin word for "thank you." There are many prayers that express our thanks to God for our food and our other blessings. A favorite "grace" is:

Bless, O God, this food to our use and us to your service, and make us ever
mindful of the needs of others; through Jesus Christ our Lord. Amen.

A very old prayer for meal times is:

Blessed are you, O Lord God, Creator of the Universe, for you give us
food to sustain our lives and make our hearts glad; through Jesus Christ
our Lord. Amen.

The next one can also be sung, to a tune called "Old Hundredth," because the music was originally written to be sung with a poetic version of Psalm 100.

Praise God from whom all blessings flow;
Praise God all creatures here below;
Praise God above ye heavenly host;
Praise Father, Son, and Holy Ghost. Amen.

Making Up Your Own Prayers

Although you can pray the prayers first spoken by other people, making up your own prayers may be best of all. You may want to have special times in the morning or at night when you tell God what is on your mind. Some people say they have a kind of "inner conversation with God" all day long. The important thing is to know that there is nothing you cannot share with God. As your best friend, God wants you to share your feelings honestly. You might find yourself praying:

God, I'm so mad. Emily was chosen to be captain of the team and I think I deserved it. Help me not to be mean to her. Amen.

Or:
God, I feel so torn apart. My mom and dad aren't getting along and may get divorced. Please take care of everybody in this family, no matter what happens.

Or:
God, I'm worried. My grandma is sick. I don't want her to die. Help me to understand that you are always with her, and with me, too. Amen.

"Asking prayer" is not the only kind of prayer, however. Perhaps we feel like saying "thank you."

O God, I love your world. Thank you for my family—my mom and dad and my dog Butch and maybe my brother. Amen.

You can also write down your own prayers, in your prayer journal. Some people write their prayers as "letters to God." You could begin "Dear God" and then tell God the things you have on your mind. God loves and understands you completely, so you can tell God everything when you are praying.

Prayers from a Youth Conference

The following prayers were written by participants in a Youth Conference in the Episcopal Diocese of New York.[5]

God, please forgive me for going the wrong way again. (Daniel Miller)

Dear God, thank you for your strength to go out and try to accomplish those things that I did not think I could achieve. (Keely Coffey)

Dear Lord, thank you for a wonderful day, even when I had no confidence. (Manny Lampan)

Father please,
Give me strength to lift my stress.
Give me speed to outrun evil.
Give me intelligence to outwit my fears.
Give me wisdom to follow my dreams. (Erik Smith)

Begin by deciding how you want to address God. Some people just say "God"; some people pray to Jesus or the Holy Spirit. Some people prefer something different, like "Holy Mystery." I like the words in the *New Zealand Prayer Book*: "Eternal Spirit, Earth-maker, Pain-bearer, Life-giver, Source of all that is and that shall be, Father and Mother of us all, Loving God, in whom is heaven."[6]

Now tell God the things you have on your mind. You might want to ask something for yourself or for someone else. You may want to confess something, and say you are sorry. You may want to thank God for something, or complain about something. Be perfectly honest. God understands you even better than you understand yourself.

End with "Amen."

Pictures and Drawings

- 3 -

Praying by Thinking about God

Just as thinking about our friends can help us to get to know them better, thinking about God can help us feel closer to God. One of the ways we can pray in this way is to think about a Bible story. People have been practicing this kind of prayer for many centuries. For example, our Hebrew ancestors liked to study the Torah—the first five books of the Bible—in this way. For them, meditating on Scripture was so nourishing and so delightful that it felt like eating honey.

> *How sweet are your words to my taste!*
> *They are sweeter than honey to my mouth.* (Psalm 119:103)

Over the centuries, various methods have been developed to help people think about Scripture. I have simplified them into a simple pattern: **prepare, picture, ponder,** and **permit.**

Let's imagine, for example, that you have chosen to think about the following story in the Gospel of Mark, chapter 4. First, **prepare** by setting aside some time to think about God. Give yourself a few minutes to become quiet and relaxed, then read the story:

On that day, when evening had come, Jesus said to his friends, "Let us go across to the other side of the lake." And leaving the crowd behind, they took him with them in the boat, just as he was. And other boats were with him. And a great storm of wind arose, and the waves beat into the boat, so that the boat was already filling. But Jesus was in the back of the boat, asleep on the cushion; and they woke him up and said to him, "Teacher, do you not care if we die?"

He woke up and rebuked the wind, and said to the sea, "Peace. Be still." Then the wind ceased, and there was a great calm. He said to them, "Why are you afraid? Have you no faith?" And they were filled with awe, and said to one another, "Who then is this, that even wind and sea obey him?"

Now **picture** the story, as if you were watching a DVD or, better still, as if you were actually there in the boat, among the apostles, maybe beside Peter. Can you "see" the waves on the lake, the small boat being tossed up and down, the terrified faces of the disciples? But do more than picture. What would your other senses pick up? Can you hear the beating of the rain, the splashing of the water, the creaking of the rigging, the shouts of the disciples? Can you feel the violent motion of the boat, the cold spray on your face, and the water rising around your ankles as it splashes into the boat? Can you feel your confusion and fear, because the power of this storm is one of the most frightening things you've ever experienced? And then how would it feel when Jesus finally awoke and calmed the storm? Would you be relieved, but also maybe a little scared at his power? Think about the questions you would ask. Just who is this person? How did he do that? Really put yourself into the story.

Then **ponder** the story. "Ponder" is a word that comes from the Latin word meaning "heavy." To ponder something is letting a thought sink down into you by asking yourself, "What does this story have to do with my life? What does it mean to me personally?" I don't know about you, but I certainly can think of times in my life when I felt as if I were in a storm. Maybe you can think of times when your family life was stormy, or when school became

overwhelming, or when your emotions felt as uncontrollable as that danger-
ous lake. You felt helpless, "seasick," and there seemed to be no escape.

Now ask yourself the question, "How can I **permit** my friendship with
God to grow, through some action inspired by the thoughts I have had about
this story?" It might be as simple a thing as making a phone call to a friend,
trying to think in a new way about someone you can't stand, or asking God
for help. This story always reminds me that, when my heart or my life feels
out of control, the best solution is to do just what the disciples did. They
called on Jesus. When we face difficult times, we are likely to find new peace
and calm when we spend some time with God in prayer. God loves us and
cares for us. Feeling that we are loved by God gives us a powerful inner
resource. Knowing that God loves you does not necessarily mean that the
storms will cease, but it does mean that you are never alone, that you will
have company to help you get through the storms—the presence of God.

Prepare, Picture, Ponder, and Permit: four little words, but a wonderful
pattern to help us think about that Presence, always with us.

There are other ways of "thinking," of course. You do not always have
to sit quietly to think about a story. Some people might like to *draw* the
story: either illustrating it literally, or trying to depict in an abstract way the
way the disciples felt before and after. Another great way to think is to
move. You can do this alone or with your friends, perhaps using green or
blue scarves for the stormy water, or being the disciples, huddled and shiv-
ering from fear, and then straightening up and breathing a sigh of relief.

Or you could *make* music. What kind of sounds can you produce, with
your voice or with instruments, that might suggest the waves, wind, and
rain? You could even make up your own song that tells the story. You could
also sing someone else's songs, maybe one like the "Navy Hymn," which
asks for God's protection for sailors on the sea.

Almighty Father, strong to save,
whose arm hath bound the restless wave,
who bidd'st the mighty ocean deep
its own appointed limits keep:

O hear us when we cry to thee
for those in peril on the sea.[7]

There is also a hymn from the Dakota Indian tribe, "Many and Great," which is fun to sing with a drum.

Many and great, O God, are thy works,
maker of earth and sky;
thy hands have set the heavens with stars;
thy fingers spread the mountains and plains:
Lo, at thy word the waters were formed;
deep seas obey thy voice.[8]

Over the years, I have made a list of my favorite stories to "think about" when I pray. Beside each story listed below is the place you can find it in the New Testament or Christian scriptures. Some of them are parables, stories that Jesus himself told to help people understand God better. Using your mind and imagination will help you understand all of these stories better. Better still, you will discover new ideas about your own friendship with God. Even though you may use no words at all, thinking is an important way of praying.

The Wedding at Cana (John 2:1–11)
The Miraculous Catch of Fish (Luke 5:1–11)
The Healing of the Paralyzed Man (Mark 2:1–12)
The Parable of the Sower (Mark 4:1–9)
The Parable of the Mustard Seed (Mark 4:30–32)
The Feeding of the Five Thousand (Mark 6:30–44)
Jesus Walking on the Water (Matthew 24:22–33)
The Parable of the Good Samaritan (Luke 10:29–37)
The Parable of the Prodigal Son (Luke 15:11–32)
Mary and Martha (Luke 10:38–42)
The Healing of Ten Lepers (Luke 17:11–19)

The Healing of Bartimaeus (Mark 10:46–52)
Zacchaeus (Luke 19:1–10)
The Good Shepherd (John 10:11–15)
Gethsemane (Mark 14:32–42)
The Crucifixion (Luke 23:33–46)
The Resurrection (Mark 16:1–8)

Choose one of the stories on the list above. Then

Prepare. Take time to read the story, and then relax, thinking about God's presence with you during this time.

Picture. Try to see and hear (and touch, taste, and smell) the story in as much detail as possible. Put yourself in the middle of the action.

Ponder. What meaning does this story have for you? Does it relate to your life in some way?

Permit. Is there something you can do to put into action the message the story has given you? This can be as simple as a prayer or a telephone call. On the other hand, it might help you make an important decision about something.

Pictures and Drawings

- 4 -

Praying by Silent Listening

One of the simplest kinds of praying is called by many names: the prayer of silent listening, centering prayer, meditation, or contemplative prayer. This is a kind of praying which you may have done all your life, but perhaps you did not know it was praying.

For example, when you have seen something very beautiful in nature, the experience may leave you speechless. Whether it is the magnificence of the Grand Canyon or the vastness of the starry sky on a clear summer night, or something incredibly delicate and complex, like the fragile beauty of a single flower blossom, you feel a sense of connection to a power and love far beyond yourself. On the other hand, when you become quiet and "dreamy," sometimes you feel that power and love within yourself, at what you might call your "center." Often these experiences come as a surprise. But there is a long tradition of Christian prayer that teaches ways of becoming quiet inside, so that you can become more open to that sense of God's loving presence within you.

Prepare

It is helpful to follow a pattern in this kind of prayer, too. It is a simple one: prepare, focus, and move beyond the focus.

I know that sometimes, when I want just to be silent in God's presence, it is as if my brain is a room full of people yelling into their cell phones. I think of things I should be doing, about someone who has hurt me, about what I'm going to eat for dinner. Thoughts keep tumbling in and spinning around in my head. So I need to prepare. I have found that some gentle exercise, like stretching, helps to quiet my body. Then I try to relax my muscles. You can do that in several ways. You can shake the tenseness out of your legs, arms, and torso. You can first tense each muscle and then relax it. Or you can just send a message—"relax"—to the parts of the body that feel tense.

Then find a position in which you can be comfortable. Some people sit in a chair, some sit on the floor or the ground, and some people even lie down. You can either close your eyes or leave your eyes partly open, but don't really look at anything.

Notice your breathing. There is something about noticing your breathing that is very calming. When I notice my breathing, I often think of a passage in the first book of the Bible, the book of Genesis. In the second chapter, there is a wonderful story that tells about God's creation of the first human being. Rather than a scientific, historical story, it is a story that explains the way we human beings experience ourselves. I will give you a rough translation from the Hebrew, with some Hebrew words in parentheses:

> *Then God took a handful of earth* (adamah) *and shaped a human form, and breathed life-breath* (ruach) *into that form, and that form became a human being* (adam).

That passage describes our experience as "adams," which actually means "earthlings." It says that our bodies are made from earth (*adamah*); they share the cycles of nature while we are on earth, and they return to earth when we die. But it also suggests that there is something within us:

the gift of life (*ruach*) that comes from our Creator. Our bodies themselves are reminders of that fact. When we feel the weight of our bodies being pulled to the earth by the power of gravity, it is a sign that we are *adamah*. When we inhale and exhale, it is a sign that God gave us life-breath (*ruach*) and keeps holding us in life. And that's what it means to be human—*adam*, which is really a pun or "play upon" the word *adamah*.

That is why I always begin my prayer time by noticing the weight of my body and noticing my breathing.

Focus

Once you get your body calmed down, it doesn't necessarily mean that your brain is calmed down. That is why we need the second part of the pattern: focus. Focusing on something helps us become quiet, so that we can move into a listening mode. It is natural for our minds to wander during this kind of prayer. When other thoughts come into your mind, just let them float past like clouds moving across the sky. Let them go, and return to your focus.

The Breath: There are lots of ways to focus. You might want to focus simply on your breathing. Try to breathe through your nose, not your mouth, and just notice your breath coming in and going out. This is especially helpful once you have made the mental connection between your breath and God's *ruach.* As you breathe, you can focus on the fact that God is always with you.

A Word: Some people find it helpful to focus on a word while they are breathing. You can choose your own word, like "God" or "Jesus" or "Peace." It can even be several words, like the line from the psalm, "Be still and know that I am God."

An Object: One of the ways I find most helpful to focus is to hold an object in my hand. I have a collection of stones from different parts of the world. My favorite one is from the Sea of Galilee, the lake where the story of the Stilling of the Storm took place. Holding that stone always stills whatever inner storms are churning around inside me. You might want to hold a stone you found in a place that's important to you, or another natural object like a pinecone from your backyard or seashell you find on vacation. Some people use a cross or prayer beads (a rosary) in this way.

An Image: There are two ways to focus on an image. One is to actually look at something, like a candle or a religious picture. The other way is to close your eyes and picture something. You might want to picture Jesus, or a beautiful church or scene from nature where you have felt the presence of God.

Sound. It is amazing how quieting it can be to focus on the sounds around you. That can be true no matter where you live. I once taught a meditation class on Forty-second Street in New York City, where the main sounds were sirens, blaring horns, racing motors, and helicopters hovering overhead. Believe it or not, once we practiced hearing those sounds as a kind of background symphony, they became a preparation for silent listening to God.

Music is probably one of the most important things in your life. Listening to music is also a wonderful way to pray. You may have special music that makes you feel quiet, like the chants from the Taizé Community in France, which you can hear on tapes or CDs.[9] Or you may be like a young friend of mine who likes to listen to hip-hop or pop to calm down.

Some people like to chant, themselves. You can chant music from Taizé, use a line of a hymn or psalm, or make up your own tunes.

Move beyond the Focus

Focusing is not the goal of this kind of prayer, however. It is only a tool to help you become silent in the presence of God. Focusing is a way to quiet the noise inside you so that you can truly listen to God.

"Listening to God" does not mean that you will necessarily hear anything. It means that you are practicing being open to God's love. That is something that you can feel more than hear. You are becoming better and better acquainted with your truest and deepest self. When you center like this, you will grow in self-acceptance, because at the very center of your being is God's *ruach*, the gift of life, God's special gift to you as a unique human being, one of a kind.

Journal Pages

Give yourself a period of ten minutes during which you will not be interrupted. Stretch your muscles, and then find a comfortable position in which you can let your body become heavy and relaxed. Now notice your breathing—in and out, in and out. Think of your breath as God's gift of life to you.

Find a word that will help you focus on your breathing and God's presence with you, like the word "God," "Jesus," "Spirit," or "holy." (You can use other "focus" ideas from this chapter instead, if you like.) When your mind wanders, as it inevitably will, just bring your attention back gently to the word or other focus.

Enjoy this time of being aware of God's love for you. You don't have to stop after ten minutes. Take as much time as you want.

What is it like to be still and try to focus on your breathing?

Did your mind wander, and were you able to bring it back again to your focus?

How did this exercise make your body feel?

What words would describe what happens in your mind and spirit?

In what ways do you think time in silence can build your friendship with God?

Pictures and Drawings

- 5 -

Praying in Work and in Play

Working Along with God

You may have already discovered how close to your friends you become when you work together on a project, like making stage sets for the school play or practicing with the marching band or the soccer team. Friendship with God can grow in the same way. When you help to make God's world a better place, this too is prayer.

Helping others is one way of doing that. There are so many examples; I will just name a few, to get your own thoughts going: visit a neighbor who is handicapped, old, or ill, or even offer to shop for them; collect clothes or food for people who need them; enter a walkathon to raise money for a good cause.

One of the ways I have decided to try to make the world a better place is to help care for the environment through my actions. I try to walk or cycle when I can, rather than using the car; to turn off lights I am not using; to pick up litter; and to buy from local farmers when I can. I have even begun to write letters to politicians to express my opinions about environmental issues. Most important of all, I try to keep learning about the ways human beings can contribute to the earth's health, rather than damaging it. There is an increasing amount of information available about how our lifestyles make an impact upon places and people who may be far away from us. SUVs, for example, consume huge amounts of gasoline and contribute to global warming. Many people (and I am one of them) think there needs to be a real change in attitude about our relationship with the natural world. Because you may be learning some up-to-date facts about this issue in school, you can help by sharing your knowledge with your family.

Journal Pages

What are some of the ways that you "work along with God," or that you
would like to in the future?

Try writing a letter to a congressperson about an issue you care deeply
about. You don't have to mail it if you don't want to, but you might
make a difference if you do!

Pictures and Drawings

Making and Doing Things

Some artists say that when they draw or paint or sculpt, it makes them feel happy and free, as if they were praying. Musicians have said the same thing about composing music, playing an instrument, or singing. The same is true for dancers, scientists, inventors, writers, and other people who use their special gifts to create things or do things. These kinds of praying are not only for people who make a living in these ways, but for everybody. You are good at doing certain things, for example. Perhaps you like to swim or play basketball or other sports. Or you like to act in plays or to help take care of younger children. Perhaps you are good at writing, drawing, or carpentry. Or maybe you love singing, playing the trumpet, or dancing. We all have gifts, and God, our Creator, loves to see us use them. When we use these gifts, they not only make us feel happy and free, but we are contributing something to the world around us.

When we recognize our own special gifts, it helps us accept the fact that we don't all have every gift. I was never good at sports like softball. When I would try to play with my brothers, I would always strike out, and I hardly ever caught the ball. In fact, one time I let it crash into my nose. I was good at playing the piano though, and doing that made me feel happy. You may wish you were good in sports, but if you are not, think about the things you are good at, things you love to do.

Some people's eyes are good at seeing softballs, but they can't play an instrument like the piano or the guitar. Some people's eyes are good at reading music, but they have a hard time seeing softballs, tennis balls, or even large basketballs coming toward them. Some people's imaginations think in pictures, and they can draw very well, but they have trouble writing things down. Some people's imaginations think in words, and they can write wonderful stories, but they have trouble drawing things. Some people are good at roller-blading, but they get impatient when they try to play video games. Some people are geniuses at video games and can barely balance on roller blades.

That doesn't mean that we shouldn't try everything that we want to:

playing softball, playing the piano, drawing, writing, rollerblading, and playing video games. Never be afraid to try something because you think you can't do it. You may surprise yourself. But always remember that we do not need to feel bad if some things are harder for us than other things.

Journal Pages

What are some things that are hard for you?

What are some things that are easy for you?

What are your special gifts?

What things make you unhappy and uncertain?

What do you learn from these feelings?

What things make you feel most happy and free? Try to describe these
feelings.

Pictures and Drawings

Learning

When you think about it, your mind is one of the most important gifts God has given you. When you take the time to follow your natural curiosity and to learn about the world around you, you probably appreciate God's world more. So, even if going to school or doing your homework doesn't always seem like growing in friendship with God, it can be.

You can learn in other ways as well, like going to museums; watching any of the dozens of programs about history, nature, and travel on cable; taking a class—maybe ballet or violin lessons, or reading books from the library. You can learn about how to plant a garden, care for pets, build a cabin, or identify birds or insects. Learning about God's interesting world makes life more fun and helps you become a more interesting human being, too.

Journal Pages

What is your favorite subject in school? Why do you like it?

Is there something outside school you like to learn about as well?

What subject do you dislike the most? Why?

Is there anything that would make you like it better?

What would you like to learn that they don't teach in school?

Can you think of ways to figure out how to do that?

Pictures and Drawings

Deciding Things

Sometimes we have to decide whether or not to do something.

Maybe some of your friends want you to join them in doing something that you know isn't right, like shoplifting. Maybe your friends make fun of a new student who has a different way of dressing or talking. You are afraid that if you are kind to that person, they may even turn against you, but you do not want to join in your friends' teasing. Maybe you want to hang out with someone your parents have forbidden you to see. Maybe it seems like the easiest thing to do is to put off doing your homework or other jobs, but you know down deep that these tasks will not go away, and you will not feel later any more like doing them than you do now.

Maybe there are people who are putting pressure on you to do things that you know are not good for you, like smoking cigarettes, drinking alcohol, or using drugs. You know, however, that, in the long run, the best way to enjoy life is not to escape your problems through getting high in these ways. You have discovered that there are better highs. Perhaps you have felt amazingly energized by exercise, or very happy and satisfied because you have helped someone. Maybe you have been awestruck by a hike through a wilderness area, or have felt God's presence with you while you were praying. These highs make you feel better after they are over, not sick or hungover.

It is sometimes very difficult to choose what you know is right for you, rather than what is easiest to do. It is hard to decide not to go along with other people. But a very important way to grow in friendship with God is to decide to do what you think is right, even if it is hard, and to do it without acting as if you were better than everybody else. Making decisions like this is a very important way of praying. And God is always there to help you.

Journal Pages

What are some of the difficult choices and decisions you have had to make?

What was it like to do something you knew you shouldn't do?

What is it like to feel pressure from other people to do things you know are not right for you?

How can your friendship with God help you when this happens?

Pictures and Drawings

Having Fun

I have always liked what a very wise man named Irenaeus (pronounced e-ruh-nay-us, with the accent on the "nay") said: "The glory of God is the human being fully alive." These words of Irenaeus, who lived in the second century, remind me that the words "praying" and "playing" are alike except for one letter. When we take time to rest and to have fun, we are, in a way, saying "thank you" to our Creator. Actually, young people are probably better at this kind of praying than adults. You may even know some adults who admit they are "workaholics," and who hardly ever take time to have fun. Praying by playing can be as simple as playing ball, hanging out with your friends, dancing to your favorite music, or even just sitting in the sun on a nice day, enjoying life.

Having fun helps us to feel more like the human beings we are created to be: "fully alive," happy, and healthy. Playing helps us to enjoy God's greatest gift to us: our life.

Journal Pages

What are your favorite things to do?

What words describe how you feel when you are playing, having fun,
  or resting?

What is it like to be with someone who can't seem to have fun?

Pictures and Drawings

- 6 -

Temples of the Holy Spirit

Caring for Our Bodies

I wrote earlier about the Creation story, in which God is pictured as a sculptor, making a human form from the earth and breathing life into it. You can find that story in Genesis 2:7. This story, although it is not science, teaches something that is true: that our bodies are holy and that the gift of life comes from God. In Genesis 1:26, there is another story, which talks about our being made in the "image" and "likeness" of God. Later, in his letter to the church in Corinth (1 Corinthians 6:19), St. Paul would say that our bodies are "temples of the Holy Spirit." Today, he would probably call them "churches" or "cathedrals" of the Holy Spirit.

If we believe that our bodies are holy, then we will want to take care of them. Some things are obviously not good for them, like sitting around all day watching TV, sitting in front of a computer for hours at a time, eating a lot of junk food, or abusing substances like alcohol, drugs, or tobacco. Taking care of our bodies helps us enjoy life, because we will feel better, both physically and mentally.

As you mature, you will notice changes in your body, and you will realize more and more that you are a sexual being. Thinking about the body as a temple helps you remember to respect not only your own body, but those of other people. You will not want to just "use" other people's bodies sexually for your own satisfaction, or let other people use yours, or be hurt by them in any way. Some people use their bodies and sex for escape, or as a way of getting a "buzz," the way others use drugs or alcohol. But if you really respect your body and those of others, you will realize that brief moments of pleasure, like all of our actions, are likely to have long-term consequences.

Speaking of respect, one of the messages of those biblical passages in the book of Genesis is that our bodies are good. One of the things I have always loved to do, whether in an airport or on the sidewalk in a busy city, is to people-watch. People come in all shapes, sizes, colors, and ages. It is obvious that God likes variety in the world, not sameness.

Often, when we look at pictures of people in the media, whether it is in magazines, movies, or on TV, we feel as if we do not measure up to the ideal image. We might wish we were thinner, taller, stronger, or even a different color. When we feel confused or depressed because of comparing ourselves to others, we can take our feelings to God in prayer. Perhaps you can even hear, in your spirit, God's voice saying, "I have created you, and you are good."

Journal Pages

Actual temples, or places of prayer, are very different from one another; like people, they come in all shapes and sizes.

How would you describe your body?

How do you feel about the way it looks?

Even if your body does not match the ads you see in magazines or on television, how can you appreciate it as God's good creation?

What are some ways you can respect and care for your body?

What are some ways you can respect the bodies of others as God's good creation?

Pictures and Drawings

Praying with our Bodies

People of many religious traditions have taught that our bodies can actually help us to pray, through the practice of certain physical disciplines. There are many ways that our bodies can help us pray, when we adopt these disciplines into our Christian faith.

One that many people find especially helpful is hatha yoga. In hatha yoga, a series of stretches and poses done with special attention to the breathing is likely to make you feel very calm and quiet inside. I like it so much, in fact, that I have written a special book about Christian yoga.[10]

On the other hand, two of my young friends are enthusiastic about tae kwondo, and tell me that it makes them feel centered and strong, so they are better able to deal with the stresses of life.

A very ancient way of prayer is called "meditation walking." In meditation walking, you walk very slowly, making sure that you have the weight solidly on your foot at each step. As you do it, you also pay attention to your breathing. It always reminds me of the importance of really being in the present moment, rather than clinging to the past or worrying about the future.

You can invent your own ways to "pray with your body." I like choosing a phrase from the Bible or the liturgy, thinking of a movement that expresses it, and doing it over and over. An example is reaching up toward the sky when I think of God as our Creator, reaching out to the sides so my body is in the shape of a cross when I think of Jesus, and reaching in toward my heart and then out again, as I think of God's Holy Spirit within me and also connecting me to the world. Maybe you also can find some phrases from Psalms that you can use to create your own body-prayer.

Do you like a sport, like swimming, cross-country skiing, cycling, or running? You may discover that it works well to pray while you are doing these things. I love to swim laps, and sometimes organize my laps by figuring out who needs my prayers. Then I do not have to remember numbers (something I am not good at); I only need to remember people.

You can act out a Bible story, alone or with others. It is a very powerful way to go beyond the words to the meaning and feeling behind the words. You can do the same thing with a familiar prayer or a Psalm. And hymns and songs are great accompaniments for movement.

There are many other kinds of exercise that you may find helpful both to keep you healthy and to remind you of your friendship with God, as a "human being fully alive." It has always been interesting to me that the words "health" and "holy" come from the same ancient word: *hal*, which means "whole." I guess it should be no surprise, then, that exercise can be part of our prayer.

Journal Pages

What kinds of exercise do you like to do?
How could it be part of your prayer?

Choose a verse from a Psalm and make up a movement that expresses it. It is fun to do a whole Psalm with a group. If you have enough people, two or three people can be assigned to each verse. You can have someone read the Psalm slowly as you move, and choose some music to play in the background. The end result is a Psalm-in-movement. What was it like for you and the others to do this?

Pictures and Drawings

- 7 -

Praying All Day Long

Most people find that special times of praying, like grace at meals or prayers at a certain time of day, help them to remember God's friendship all day long.

When you wake up in the morning, you can thank God for the new day, and ask God to help you in everything you do that day.

When you go to bed, you can think about your day and ask God to forgive you for any wrong things you wish you hadn't done. You can ask God to help you avoid doing them again. You can ask God to watch over people you care about; you may even wish to keep a list of those people, so that you will remember them all. You can pray for peace in the world. You can ask for help with any problems you have. You can thank God for all your blessings—especially for life. Bedtime is a special time for talking with God, thinking about God, and quiet listening.

At special prayer times, some people like to kneel with heads bowed and hands folded, but that certainly is not the only way to pray. You can also pray standing up, with your arms stretched out, or sit cross-legged on the floor with your hands on your knees. Some people like to pray sitting in a chair with their hands in their lap. You can find the position in which you feel best. You can pray kneeling, sitting, standing, or lying down. You can pray walking, you can pray dancing, you can pray singing, you can pray working, you can pray playing.

Is it beginning to seem as if your entire life can be "praying"? You are very lucky if you can begin to understand this now, because many people don't understand it, even when they are quite old. They think that praying is only saying some words. But now you know that prayer is everything we do that helps us grow in friendship with God: talking, thinking, moving, deciding, working, making, playing, just being—everything.

Amen.

What kinds of prayer in this book especially appeal to you? What makes them appealing?

Do you have your own ideas about prayer? I'd like to hear about them, or try to answer any questions you may have. My e-mail is **RevNancyRoth@aol.com,** and you can get to know me better at my Web site: **www.revnancyroth.org**.

_____

_____

_____

_____

_____

_____

_____

_____

_____

_____

_____

_____

_____

Pictures and Drawings

Notes

1. *The Saint Helena Psalter*, copyright 2004 by the Order of St. Helena (New York: Church Publishing Incorporated). Used by permission.

2. All published by HarperSanFrancisco in 1991, 1992, and 1996, respectively.

3. *The Oxford Book of Prayer* (Oxford: Oxford University Press, 1985).

4. Elisabeth Roberts and Elios Amidon, eds. *Earth Prayers From Around the World: 365 Prayers, Poems, and Invocations for Honoring the Earth.* (San Francisco: Harper, 1991), 95.

5. Reprinted by permission of the Episcopal Diocese of New York.

6. *The New Zealand Prayer Book* (London: Collins Liturgical Publications, 1989), 181.

7. *The Hymnal* 1982 (New York: The Church Pension Fund, 1985), Hymn 579.

8. Ibid., Hymn 385.

9. Available from G.I.A. Publications, 7404 South Mason Avenue, Chicago, IL 60638.

10. Nancy Roth, *Invitation to Christian Yoga* (Available 2005 from Church Publishing Incorprated.)